D0862854

HAPPY BIRTHDAY YOU
OLD FART!

Written By:
Herbert Kavet

Illustrated By:
Martin Riskin

Manufactured in the United States of America

30 29 28 27 26 25 24 23 22 21 20 19 18 17 16 15 14 13 12 11 10 9 8 7 6 5 4 3 2

Ivory Tower Publishing Co., Inc.
125 Walnut St., P.O. Box 9132, Watertown, MA 02272-9132
Telephone #: (617) 923-1111   Fax #: (617) 923-8839

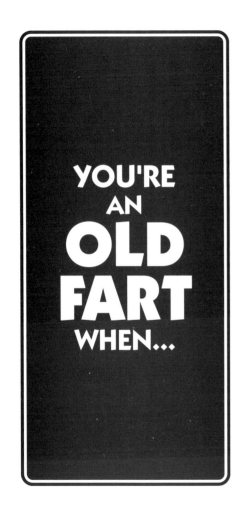

YOU'RE AN OLD FART WHEN...

You leave programming the VCR to people under 25. You wonder if you can stall becoming computer literate until retirement. If you memorize a few key computer buzz words, would it fool the "kids" at work?

You may straddle two lanes, but you no longer
get speeding tickets.

YOU'RE AN OLD FART WHEN...

You can still read fine print provided there is enough light and magnifying glasses are available.

You know where all your warranties are. Unfortunately, you probably can't find your glasses so you can read them.

YOU'RE AN OLD FART WHEN...

You no longer have any illusions about making it big in your job. You fantasize less and less about going into your own business.

You're smart enough not to take out all the garbage in one trip.

YOU'RE AN OLD FART WHEN...

You are just starting to use your age to elicit extra services.
You no longer feel funny when college-age people call
you Mr. or Ma'am.

Your pets are finally trained to obey your instructions.

YOU'RE AN OLD FART WHEN...

YOU'RE AN OLD FART WHEN...

There is no stopping the growth of hair in your ears and nose or on your chest and chin. You finally realize you've stopped growing taller though there is plenty of expansion sideways. There's no growth, however, on your head.

You don't care where your wife goes when she goes out,
as long as you don't have to go with her.

YOU'RE
AN
OLD
FART
WHEN...

YOU'RE AN OLD FART WHEN...

You hurt after participating in almost any physical activity. Often you hurt after doing absolutely nothing at all. You're glad to read that taking aspirin also prevents various horrible diseases because you swallow an awful lot of them.

You dress for comfort rather than in the latest style.

YOU'RE AN OLD FART WHEN...

YOU'RE AN OLD FART WHEN...

You spend less and less time between visits to a toilet. You stop more often on car trips and frequently make nighttime pilgrimages.

You finally learn which foods are incompatible with your gastrointestinal system.

YOU'RE AN OLD FART WHEN...

You're smart enough to save out-of-style clothing
until it becomes fashionable again.

You no longer can sleep until noon.
Probably you can't sleep much past dawn.

YOU'RE
AN
OLD
FART
WHEN...

YOU'RE AN OLD FART WHEN...

You don't care nearly as much about what people think of your dress or behavior. You've pretty much adopted a style you like and people can go to hell if they don't like it.

Your mind is as sharp as ever and you never forget the really important things.

YOU'RE AN OLD FART WHEN...

Your biological urges may be slowing a bit but you're just as interested in looking as ever. If you're a man, you don't wake up "aroused" everyday.

You finally understand the dangers of too much sun
and take steps to guard against overexposure.

You no longer break out in hives when you have to speak before a group.

Not only do you have trouble going upstairs, but when you get there, you may have forgotten what you went upstairs for.

You know more about fixing things than the people they send to repair them.

You've resigned yourself to never owning that big waterfront lot or a helicopter or achieving some great artistic or scientific accomplishment. And you don't mind much because you're pretty satisfied just as you are.

You can't fool your stomach with a pastrami sandwich
or cream pie just before bedtime.

You plan ahead to be able to read menus in candlelit restaurants. You learn to avoid places with menus printed in small red type on a maroon background.

YOU'RE AN **OLD FART** WHEN...

YOU'RE AN OLD FART WHEN...

You start arranging your hair rather than just combing it.
Your bathroom is filled with exotic shaped bottles promising
all sorts of miracles with your hair. None of them work.

You stop to think and sometimes forget to start again.

YOU'RE
AN
OLD
FART
WHEN...

Your kids are earning more than you.

You probably have started experimenting with a few sex aids.

YOU'RE AN OLD FART WHEN...

It takes you days to find suits that show enough skin while covering all the bad parts. You've reached a level of maturity that allows you to ignore short-lived fashion fads.

You are always the "designated" driver.

YOU'RE AN **OLD FART** WHEN...

YOU'RE AN OLD FART WHEN...

You've reached some sort of accord with your maker even if it's only to add "God willing" to the end of most of your statements.

You can afford to vacation in really exotic places.

You act your age... most of the time.

You can still wear out most kids at your favorite sport.

YOU'RE
AN
**OLD
FART**
WHEN...

No one knows what to buy you.

You're an animal until you've had your morning coffee.
A morning without coffee is worse than constipation.
You're not sure you are a member of the human race
until you've had a big cupful.

YOU'RE
AN
OLD
FART
WHEN...

YOU'RE AN OLD FART WHEN...

You never really had the chance to get used to guys with long hair or earrings. Sometimes you have trouble doing your business at times like this.

You can handle steamy movies with aplomb.

YOU'RE AN OLD FART WHEN...

YOU'RE AN OLD FART WHEN...

Young people accept you as an equal.

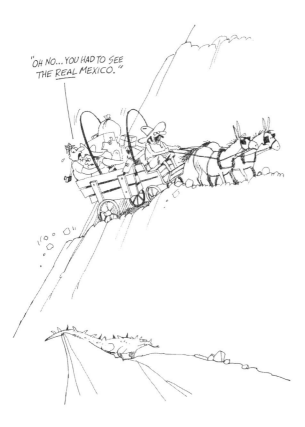

You prefer vacations that involve hot showers and flush toilets. You also prefer places that don't require inoculations for weird diseases.

YOU'RE AN OLD FART WHEN...

You are absolutely indispensable at your job.

The stress of having dinner with little kids is only a nostalgic memory. Grandchildren, of course, are fine for a day or two.

YOU'RE AN OLD FART WHEN...

You take your morning bathroom routine very seriously and do not like to be rushed. You think getting a little action means your prune juice is working.

You still look pretty good in a bathing suit.

YOU'RE AN OLD FART WHEN...

You don't take any crap from sales clerks. You can calmly handle most of life's emergencies. Surly waiters, phone solicitors, and incompetent sales help are a piece of cake for you.

You have a home worth 4 times what you paid for it.

YOU'RE
AN
**OLD
FART**
WHEN...

YOU'RE AN OLD FART WHEN...

You're so valuable at work you can say anything to the boss you'd like.

Your family and friends have finally identified you as the mystery farter.

YOU'RE AN **OLD FART** WHEN...

YOU'RE AN OLD FART WHEN...

Driving on dark rainy nights is something you try to avoid.
You notice your kids hesitate before driving with you.

You grow content with your weight after failing
with every fad diet to come along.

YOU'RE
AN
**OLD
FART**
WHEN...

YOU'RE AN OLD FART WHEN...

You tend to refer to anyone under 40 as a "kid".

You can't remember when things like bran and fiber weren't a regular part of your diet. Your personal plumbing needs more and more stimulation from various heavily advertised regulating remedies.

YOU'RE AN OLD FART WHEN...

You're smart enough to pace yourself to finish things you start.

YOU'RE AN OLD FART WHEN...

People start telling you "You're not getting older, you're getting better..." and you believe them.

YOU'RE AN OLD FART WHEN...

Your own kids ask you for advice—and then follow it.

You finally learn to use your bifocals, though going down steps or reading small print up high is still pretty dicey. Usually you can see fine, provided the light is good, but you no longer laugh at the idea of large print books.

YOU'RE AN OLD FART WHEN...

You feel like the "morning after" and you can swear
you haven't been anywhere.

You keep forgetting. You surround yourself with calendars, memo books and notes and still you forget.

YOU'RE AN OLD FART WHEN...

You can finally afford all the things you no longer want.

You have the maturity to realize that any really good presents are going to have to be bought by yourself.

YOU'RE AN OLD FART WHEN...

You have achieved the ability, through long years of practice, to totally and at any time tune out your marriage partner.

You don't take any baloney from haughty wine stewards or incompetent waiters.

YOU'RE AN OLD FART WHEN...

You become an expert on the weather. You watch the weather channel and carefully plan your attire for the expected conditions. You advise all your distant friends and relatives exactly what the weather is in <u>their</u> city.

Many of the things you threw out the last time you moved now turn out to be collectors' items.

You are more and more willing to experiment with unusual foods. Pizza and hamburger have given way to yogurt and tofu (did you know that tofu means "whale snot" in Japanese?). You carry antacid pills everywhere you go.

Your calendar is filled with doctor and dentist appointments.
You prefer calendars with big numbers rather than naked girls.

YOU'RE AN OLD FART WHEN...

You've stopped smoking, drink with moderation, and eat more sensibly. Still, you have to carry antacid pills around with you.

YOU'RE
AN
OLD
FART
WHEN...

Your arms aren't long enough to hold your reading material.

YOU'RE AN OLD FART WHEN...

You understand the comfort and practicality
of double-knit polyester.

Reunions with friends or old neighbors are really emotionally poignant occasions. You're pretty sure some of the reminiscences are actually better than the originals. You even start to enjoy family get-togethers.

YOU'RE AN OLD FART WHEN...

You no longer fantasize about going to nude beaches.

You're smart enough to hire a kid to mow the lawn and shovel the snow.

YOU'RE AN OLD FART WHEN...

You always look forward to changing into something loose and soft. You no longer discard out-of-style clothes because you know they usually come back. You remember that your father always wore a hat.

YOU'RE AN **OLD FART** WHEN...

You're always cold. While you wear sweaters, kids are running about almost naked and you can't believe they're not freezing.

YOU'RE AN OLD FART WHEN...

You don't see anything humorous or strange in carefully perusing any ads promising relief from hemorrhoids, constipation, hair loss, or back pain.

You have become such an expert in a specific hobby or interest that you can absolutely bore anyone to death talking about it.

YOU'RE AN OLD FART WHEN...

You know which plants can make it under your touch and which cannot.

Partying involves baked brie and white wine a lot more than waking up with your head in the toilet.

YOU'RE AN **OLD FART** WHEN...

YOU'RE AN OLD FART WHEN...

People complain about your snoring.

Everyone has already heard all your jokes. Likewise all the stories of your athletic exploits as a youth, army adventures, great romances, insightful predictions, and noble gestures have already bored most acquaintances several times over. Unfortunately you can't quite remember telling these stories to everyone, so you repeat them whenever the opportunity arises.

YOU'RE AN OLD FART WHEN...

You start to look forward to dull evenings at home.

You've gotten very, very good at your job. You even have started to make some real contributions in your field.

YOU'RE AN OLD FART WHEN...

You can no longer sleep till noon but you can sleep through most any sermon.

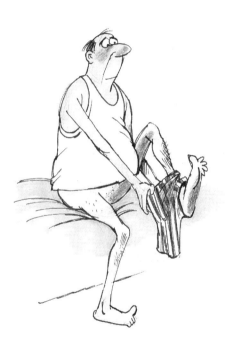

You sit down to put on your underwear, and you find the boxer style more comfortable than the jockey.

YOU'RE AN OLD FART WHEN...

Just when you were starting to learn the names of all those funny African countries, Eastern Europe and the Soviet Union split apart into even more unpronounceable little places. You have no intention of learning them until they settle down.

You remember to call girls "women" about half of the time.

YOU'RE
AN
OLD
FART
WHEN...

YOU'RE AN OLD FART WHEN...

You're back goes out more than you do. You go to doctors, osteopaths, chiropractors, and orthopedic surgeons. You change your mattress, shoes, posture, car seats. You lose weight, wear a brace, rest in bed, hang upside down, and it still hurts.

You no longer look forward to birthdays. The years skip by at a capricious pace and if the next five years pass as quickly as the last, you'll be really old sometime next week.

YOU'RE
AN
OLD
FART
WHEN...

Other books we publish are available at many fine stores. If you can't find them, send directly to us. $7.00 postpaid

2400-How To Have Sex On Your Birthday. Finding a partner, special birthday sex positions, kinky sex on your birthday and much more.

2402-Confessions From The Bathroom. There are things in this book that happen to all of us that none of us ever talk about. The Gas Station Dump, for example, or the Corn Niblet Dump, the Porta Pottie Dump and more.

2403-The Good Bonking Guide. Bonking is a great new British term for doing "you know what". Covers bonking in the dark, bonking all night long, improving your bonking, and everything else you've ever wanted to know.

2407-40 Happens. When being out of prune juice ruins your whole day and you realize anyone with the energy to do it on a weeknight must be a sex maniac.

2408-30 Happens. When you take out a lifetime membership at your health club, and you still wonder when the baby fat will finally disappear.

2409-50 Happens. When you remember when "made in Japan" meant something that didn't work, and you can't remember what you went to the top of the stairs for.

2411-The Geriatric Sex Guide. It's not his mind that needs expanding; and you're in the mood now, but by the time you're naked, you won't be!

2412-Golf Shots. What excuses to use to play through first, ways to distract your opponent, and when and where a true golfer is willing to play.

2414-60 Happens. When your kids start to look middle-aged, when software is some kind of comfortable underwear, and when your hearing is perfect if everyone would just stop mumbling.

2416-The Absolutely Worst Fart Book. The First Date Fart, The Oh My God Don't Let Me Fart Now Fart, The Lovers' Fart, The Doctor's Exam Room Fart and many more.

2417-Women Over 30 Are Better Because... Their nightmares about exams are starting to fade and their handbags can sustain life for about a week with no outside support whatsoever.

2418-9 Months In The Sac. A humorous look at pregnancy through the eyes of the baby, such as: why do pregnant women have to go to the bathroom as soon as they get to the store, and why does baby start doing aerobics when it's time to sleep?

2419-Cucumbers Are Better Than Men Because... Cucumbers are always ready when you are and cucumbers will never hear "yes, yes" when you're saying "NO, NO."

2421-Honeymoon Guide. Every IMPORTANT thing to know about the honeymoon — from The Advantages Of Undressing With The Light On (it's slightly easier to undo a bra) to What Men Want Most (being allowed to sleep right afterwards without having to talk about love).

2422-Eat Yourself Healthy. Calories only add up if the food is consumed at a table. Snacking and stand up nibbling don't count. Green M&M's are full of the same vitamins found in broccoli and lots of other useful eating information your mother never told you.

2423-Is There Sex After 40? Your wife liked you better when the bulge above your waist used to be the bulge in your trousers. You think wife-swapping means getting someone else to cook for you.

2424-Is There Sex After 50? Going to bed early just means a chance to catch up on your reading or watch a little extra t.v., and you find that you actually miss trying to make love quietly so as not to wake the children.

2425-Women Over 40 Are Better Because... Over 90 reasons why women over 40 really are better: They realize that no matter how many sit-ups and leg raises they do, they cannot recapture their 17-year-old figures—but they can find something attractive in any 21-year-old guy.

2426-Women Over 50 Are Better Because... More reasons why women over 50 are better: They will be amused if you take them parking, and they know that being alone is better than being with someone they don't like.

2427-You Know You're Over The Hill When... You tend to repeat yourself. All the stories of your youth have already bored most acquaintances several times over. Even worse, you've resigned to being slightly overweight after trying every diet that has come along in the last 15 years.

2428-Beer Is Better Than Women Because (Part II)...A beer doesn't get upset if you call it by the wrong name; and after several beers, you can roll over and go to sleep without having to talk about love.

2429-Married To A Computer. You're married to a computer if you fondle it daily, you keep in touch when you're travelling and you stare at it a lot without understanding it. You even eat most

meals with it. Truly advanced computers are indistinguishable from coke machines.

2430-Is There Sex After 30? By the time you're 30, parking isn't as much fun as it was in high school. He thinks foreplay means parading around nude in front of the mirror, holding his stomach in; and she has found that the quickest way to get rid of an unwanted date is to start talking about commitment.

2431-Happy Birthday You Old Fart! You're an Old Fart when you spend less and less time between visits to a toilet, your back goes out more than you do, you tend to refer to anyone under 40 as a "kid," and you leave programming the VCR to people under 25.

2432-Big Weenies. Why some people have big weenies while other people have teenie weenies; how to find big weenies in a strange town; rating a weenie; as well as the kinds of men who possess a putz, a prong, a schwanz, a member, a rod and a wang—and more!

2433-Games You Can Play With Your Pussy. Why everyone should have a pussy; how to give a pussy a bath (grease the sides of the tub so it won't be able to claw its way out); dealing with pussy hairs (shellac it so the hairs stay right where they belong); and everything else you ever wanted to know about pussies.

2434-Sex And Marriage. What wives want out of marriage (romance, respect and a Bloomingdale's Charge Card); what husbands want out of marriage (to be left alone when watching football games and to be allowed to go to sleep after sex).

Ivory Tower Publishing Co., Inc., 125 Walnut St., P.O. Box 9132, Watertown, MA 02272-9132   Tel: (617) 923-1111